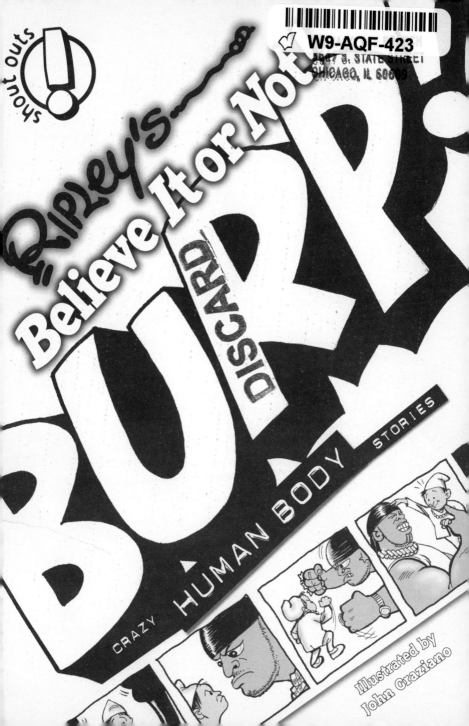

shout outs

Ripley's—
Believe It or Not!

BURP!

DISCARD

CRAZY HUMAN BODY STORIES

Illustrated by
John Graziano

PUBLISHING

Publishing Director Anne Marshall

Editorial Director Becky Miles

Art Director Sam South

Senior Designer Michelle Foster

Assistant Editor Charlotte Howell

Designer Ark Creative

Reprographics Juice Creative

Published by Scholastic Inc. SCHOLASTIC and associated logos are trademarks and/or
registered trademarks of Scholastic Inc., 557 Broadway, New York , NY 10012

ISBN 978-0-545-38078-2

12 11 10 9 8 7 6 5 4 3 2 1   12 13 14 15 16 17/0

Printed in the U.S.A.   40
First printing, January 2012

PUBLISHER'S NOTE
While every effort has been made to verify the accuracy of the entries in this book,
the Publisher cannot be held responsible for any errors contained in the work.
They would be glad to receive any information from readers.

WARNING
Some of the stunts and activities in this book are undertaken by experts and should
not be attempted by anyone without adequate training and supervision.

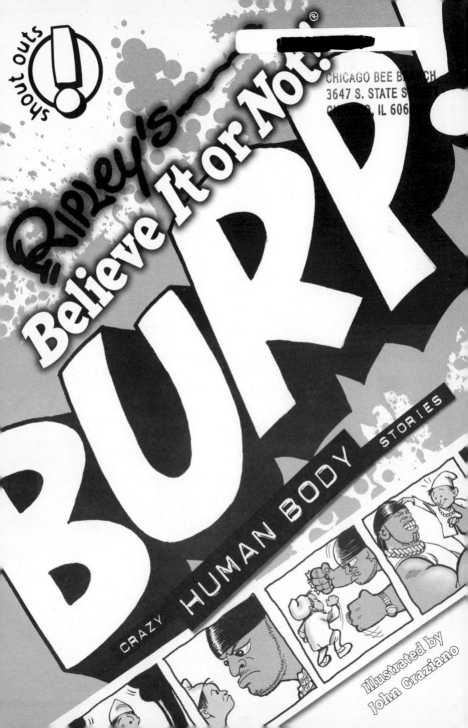

Ripley's—
Believe It or Not!

BURP!

CRAZY HUMAN BODY STORIES

Illustrated by
John Graziano

INTRODUCING...
JOHN GRAZIANO

John, Ripley's very own cartoonist, has drawn every cartoon in this wacky book of human body stories and facts.

A new Ripley's cartoon has been produced every day for the past 90 years by a dedicated Ripley's cartoonist. John is only the eighth person to take on this role. Amazingly, he got himself the job 25 years after sending his drawings to Ripley's as a teenager!

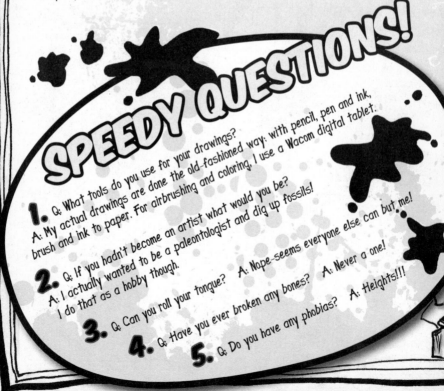

SPEEDY QUESTIONS!

1. Q: What tools do you use for your drawings?
A: My actual drawings are done the old-fashioned way: with pencil, pen and ink, brush and ink to paper. For airbrushing and coloring, I use a Wacom digital tablet.

2. Q: If you hadn't become an artist what would you be?
A: I actually wanted to be a paleontologist and dig up fossils! I do that as a hobby though.

3. Q: Can you roll your tongue?   A: Nope-seems everyone else can but me!

4. Q: Have you ever broken any bones?   A: Never a one!

5. Q: Do you have any phobias?   A: Heights!!!

HOW TO DRAW A...
SKELETON

1. Let's start creating the skeleton outline by drawing a mixture of circles and ovals. Use a pencil so you can erase the lines you don't want later. Try to match the drawing but don't worry if it isn't perfect.

2. Using the circles add the bone shapes in the right places. Some of them are funny shapes so try to copy them as best you can. Don't you think the pelvis looks like a butterfly? For help with where all the bones go see if you can remember the song: "The hip bone's connected to the back bone."

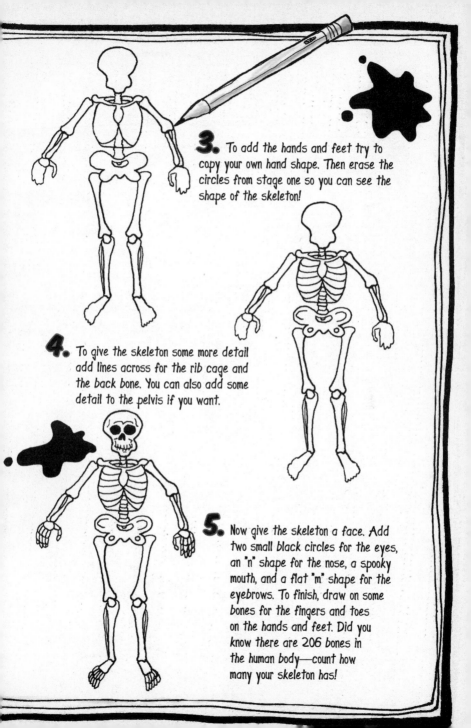

3. To add the hands and feet try to copy your own hand shape. Then erase the circles from stage one so you can see the shape of the skeleton!

4. To give the skeleton some more detail add lines across for the rib cage and the back bone. You can also add some detail to the pelvis if you want.

5. Now give the skeleton a face. Add two small black circles for the eyes, an "n" shape for the nose, a spooky mouth, and a flat "m" shape for the eyebrows. To finish, draw on some bones for the fingers and toes on the hands and feet. Did you know there are 206 bones in the human body—count how many your skeleton has!

Go to www.ripleybooks.com for more amazing facts

BURP!

human body

You won't believe how amazing the human body is when you open up this fun-packed book! Meet the boy who was saved from death by his ears, the woman who can pop her eyes out of their sockets, plus many more! It's Ripley's Shout Outs!

Super-sized body builder, Tiny Iron, has bulging biceps that measure 24 inches around—they're England's biggest biceps! That's also 2 inches more than the height of the world's smallest person, Khagendra Thapa Magar from Nepal. He's 18 years old but only 22 inches tall. The two met at a Ripley's book launch in 2010, where Khagendra was small enough to sit on Tiny Iron's open hand.

SONIC SIGHT

Lucas Murray from England has been blind since birth, but he has learned how to use a technique called echolocation to find his way around. Like a bat, he can make clicking sounds and judge the distance, size, and direction of objects around him by listening to the echoes. Now he can use the playground, go rock climbing, and even play basketball by clicking to find the hoop and throw the ball in the right direction.

The human body is made up of about one trillion cells. Our galaxy is made up of over one billion stars—roughly 1,000 times fewer stars than cells!

Mouth almighty

Stand well back when Gordon du Cane yawns or shouts—you might get swallowed up by accident! His huge mouth is more than 2 inches bigger than a baseball. He can fit a whole apple inside without it even touching the edges!

MOM IN A MILLION

Nicky Owen from England keeps seeing double—in her own family! Nicky is an identical twin, and gave birth to her own set of identical twin boys in 1996. In 2003 she had another set of twins, at odds of over 11 million to one.

The heart pumps blood around your body so hard it could squirt it 30 feet across the room!

SUPERHUMANS...

Hand-some!

Hussain Bisad has a growth condition that makes him larger than most men: His hands are 10½ inches long and he has size 26 feet.

Strong stomach

Your stomach contains hydrochloric acid to help break down the food you eat. This acid is so strong it could even dissolve a small piece of metal!

DON'T TRY THIS AT HOME!

WOW!

Coming and going

Every minute, about 3 billion of the body's cells die and are replaced. Don't panic—the body has around a trillion cells in total.

Toes up

Don't let the little things get in your way—things like losing a thumb, for instance. That happened to Englishman Peter Morris, who lost his thumb in an accident. To solve the problem, doctors removed his big toe and sewed it in the place of his severed thumb.

AMAZING!

Big shot

Basketball player Brad Millard is nicknamed "Big Continent" for his huge size. He's 7 feet 3 inches tall, weighs over 320 pounds, and has size 23 feet.

Toe-curlingly tall

Louise Hollis of California has such long toenails that it takes more than two bottles of nail polish to paint them! She doesn't cut her nails, and they are so long (over 6 inches) that she has to wear sandals with platform soles to stop them from scraping along the ground.

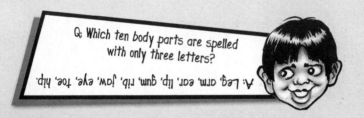

Q: Which ten body parts are spelled with only three letters?

A: Leg, arm, ear, lip, gum, rib, jaw, eye, toe, hip.

Tiny tree

Artyom Sidorkin had been suffering from extreme pains in his chest. When surgeons took a look inside, they found a 2-inch-long spruce tree growing inside his lungs! The only theory they could come up with was that the Russian man had inhaled a seed that had managed to take root and grow.

OUCH!

RUBBER BOY

A contortionist is someone who is extra bendy and can twist their body into impossible-looking positions. Often it's because their spine bones (vertebrae) are farther apart than normal, and the ligaments between them are longer and more flexible.

SQUEEZE

EXTRA BENDY

TWIST

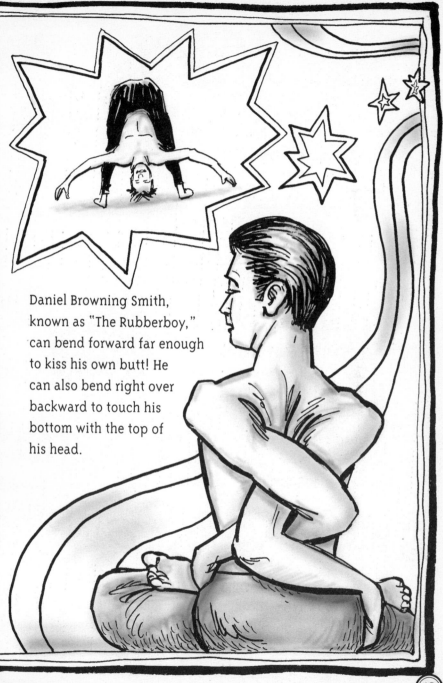

Daniel Browning Smith, known as "The Rubberboy," can bend forward far enough to kiss his own butt! He can also bend right over backward to touch his bottom with the top of his head.

FISHY CURE

Calling all asthma sufferers... imagine a fish that can cure your ailments! Every June thousands of people visit the Goud family of India to get free treatment. It's a hard cure to swallow—a herbal medicine is stuffed into a

Around 400 pints of liquid are filtered through your kidneys each day.

3-INCH-LONG FISH

which has to be eaten alive! The patients are encouraged to gulp down the wriggling fish, and the medicine is thus circulated throughout the body.

Golden oldie

And you thought your mom was old:
Omkali Charan Singh was

70 WHEN SHE GAVE BIRTH

to twins in 2008. The birth of the baby boy
and girl took place in India, and made Omkali
the oldest mother in the world. The twins were
born, and the elderly couple had two more
children to go with their grown up daughters
and six grandchildren.

Stretchy veins

If you joined together and stretched out all the blood vessels in the human body, they would be long enough to reach twice around the world.

Look out! Leonard Traenkenschuh from Washington has 3½-inch-long eyebrows!

Brilliant burper Paul Hunn from England has the world's loudest belch. It reaches

118.1 DECIBELS

or the same as a road drill, or an airplane taking off. He also performs burp routines and can speak with his belches. It may be "only natural" like he says, but Paul has practiced his technique so much that very few people can burp as loud as he can.

STICK WITH ME!

Malaysian Liew Thow has been nicknamed "Magnet Man," because metal simply sticks to him! The 71-year-old can attach cutlery, tools, and nuts and bolts to his chest, and lift heavy weights on a metal plate attached to his stomach. He's even pulled a car that was fastened to a plate on his chest! Doctors say he's not actually magnetic, but his skin has a special suction effect that makes the metal stick— as does the skin of his three sons and two grandchildren.

Chas Cheer was famous in the 1930s as the man with the xylophone head. By opening and closing his mouth while tapping on his skull, he could form different notes.

Ear, hear!

Janet Craven from England had no ears when she was born. She was unable to hear until she reached her forties, when amazing surgery changed her life. She was given a pair of

SILICONE EARS

and a hearing aid attached to the bones in her head. At first, Janet was shocked by the sound of her own voice, and fascinated by new sounds like the wind blowing in the trees.

A person living to old age will have processed up to 24 million images of their surroundings.

GOING TO
BIG SCHOOL

Any school will seem big to tiny Jyoti Amge from India because of a genetic condition that keeps her bones small. At age 16, she measured only

23½ INCHES

and had to have a separate, smaller desk alongside her classmates. She weighed around 2 pounds at birth, growing to only 11 pounds by her teens—but she still loves fashion and being the center of attention.

Great extent

Augusta Bunge from Wisconsin is a great-great-great-great-grandmother! That's seven generations covered between her and her great-great-great-great-grandson Christopher, born in 1989.

Every second, three new babies are born in the world.

HAIRY SCARY

Forget about Rapunzel—Justin Shaw from Kentucky wants to be famous for his long, silky blond hair. There's just one difference—it grows from his forearms! Justin is so proud of his long locks, he wants all the world to see them and would never dream of cutting them. At present, they're 5¾ inches, but moving to sunny Miami seems to have brought on a growth spurt!

ODDINARY FOLK...

High-brow music

F.G. Holt from Arkansas could control his face muscles so well that he could ring different bells attached to his eyebrows and play musical tunes.

WOW!

Aaatchoo!

Sneezing is no laughing matter, especially if you're Donna Griffiths from England. During the early 1980s she sneezed for 978 days without stopping. To start with, she sneezed every minute, clocking up over half a million "aaatchoos" in the first year. Later on, she sneezed every five minutes, but she still didn't find it much fun.

Say what?

Twins often communicate more closely with each other than with the outside world, but Luke and Jack Ryan have taken it a step further. The identical four-year-olds have their own language, consisting of made-up words that only the two of them understand.

A normal person eats around 60,000 pounds of food in their lifetime. That's the weight of around six elephants!

Hearing red

Don't try this at home! Long ago, French people thought that deafness could be cured by pouring a mole's blood into a deaf person's ear.

Strong boy

At just three years old, Liam Hoekstra from Michigan was smaller than average, but he was strong enough to carry furniture and lift 5-pound weights. He has a rare condition that gives him 40 percent more muscle mass than average, and hardly any body fat. He needs constant energy boosts to help his metabolism and eats six meals a day.

Alexandre Patty invented "cranial hopping," which is the art of climbing up stairs standing on your head.

AMAZING!

Itty-bitty bone

What's the smallest bone in your body? It's the teeny tiny staples, or stirrup, bone of the middle ear, and measures only 0.11 inches long.

Air-raising

If you stretched out all of your alveoli (the tiny air sacs in your lungs) they would cover a tennis court.

Some fascinating famous phobias for you:

Madonna
is afraid of thunder (known as brontophobia)

Johnny Depp
is afraid of clowns (called clourophobia)

Daniel Radcliffe
also hates clowns

Andre Agassi and Justin Timberlake
are both frightened of spiders (arachnophobia)

Sheryl Crow
is afraid of heights (acrophobia)

Paris Hilton
is afraid of small spaces (claustrophobia)

Orlando Bloom
has a fear of pigs (swinophobia)

Christina Ricci
is afraid of houseplants (botanophobia)

Chris Brown from England had a twig caught in his lung, which finally came out after 20 years when he coughed it up.

LONGER AND LONGER

Don't trip over your beard! It's a possibility for Shibsankar Bharati who lives in Calcutta, India. He hasn't cut or shaved his beard for

20 YEARS

and it now reaches an amazing 6 feet 8 inches, easily touching the floor.

Mega memory

Ask Jill Price from California where she was on any date since 1980 and she could tell you—as well as list what she ate, whom she met, what day of the week it was, and what happened in the news. Strangely, though, when she was studied by scientists, they asked her to close her eyes and she couldn't even remember what clothes they were wearing.

One human hair is strong enough to hold $3\frac{1}{2}$ ounces, which means someone with the regular 120,000 hairs on their head could support two elephants!

Big break

Can you imagine walking around with a broken leg for

That's what happened to Roy Calloway from Wales. He had been in pain ever since a motorbike accident in 1958. When he got a new X-ray in 2008, it showed that his leg hadn't healed properly when it was set all those years ago.

EAR WE GO!

Ready... aim... fire! Monte Pierce can fire coins with his earlobes, earning him the nickname "Slingshot Ears."

Monte used to pull at his lobes, pulling them longer and longer, making them stretch like elastic.

Now they hang down an inch, but he can stretch them to 5 inches...

to launch things with them. He can propel a dime over 11½ feet!

He can also pull his earlobes over his eyes...

and roll them up to stuff in his own ears!

How clean are you?

Even if you just showered, your body is covered in bacteria. Every square inch of your legs has around 8,000 bacteria, and nearly two million live on your face! Ugh—are you starting to itch?

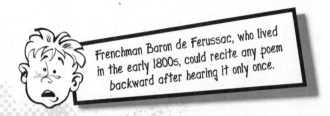

Frenchman Baron de Ferussac, who lived in the early 1800s, could recite any poem backward after hearing it only once.

IN A TWIST

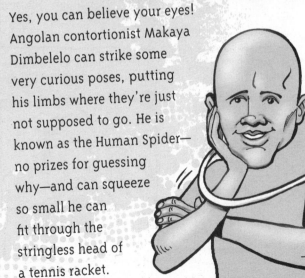

Yes, you can believe your eyes! Angolan contortionist Makaya Dimbelelo can strike some very curious poses, putting his limbs where they're just not supposed to go. He is known as the Human Spider—no prizes for guessing why—and can squeeze so small he can fit through the stringless head of a tennis racket.

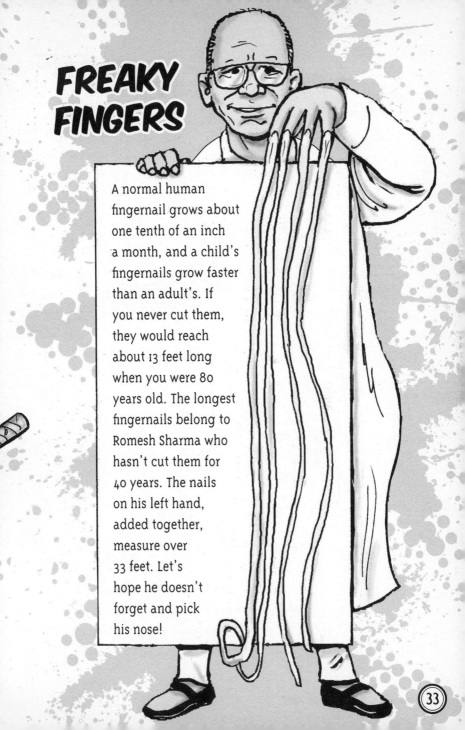

FREAKY FINGERS

A normal human fingernail grows about one tenth of an inch a month, and a child's fingernails grow faster than an adult's. If you never cut them, they would reach about 13 feet long when you were 80 years old. The longest fingernails belong to Romesh Sharma who hasn't cut them for 40 years. The nails on his left hand, added together, measure over 33 feet. Let's hope he doesn't forget and pick his nose!

BALD IS BEAUTIFUL

That's the boast of many men who are losing their hair... including the 35,000 members of the Bald Headed Men of America society. It is run by John Capps, who began

GOING BALD AT AGE 15.

The smooth operators meet up every year for the Bald is Beautiful Convention held in Morehead City, North Carolina. Morehead = less hair—get it?!

Which grows faster: fingernails or toenails?

Fingernails: nearly four times faster!

Feeling gassy?

There's a reason for that—it's called digestion. Your intestines are full of bacteria that break down the food you eat, leaving behind a whole load of gas. The gas can mostly be absorbed by your insides, but any that's left has to escape through your mouth or your bottom. Excuse you!

BODY BONANZA...

What a mouthful

Your mouth is full of germs—in fact, more germs than in any other part of your body. They have a job to do, getting rid of the leftover morsels of food. They are so tiny that 100 million workers camp out there, which is more than the combined population of California, New York, Texas, Florida, and New Jersey!

YUK!

Size for size, the brain needs A LOT more energy than your other organs—between five and ten times more.

Hair-raising

Heard any horror stories about your hair standing on end? Well, it really does! It's your body's defenses trying to make you look taller and scarier.

ZZZ-Mail

A lady sent three emails in her sleep! She turned on her computer, entered her username and password, and wrote and sent three emails, all without realizing what she had done. She knew about them only when she got replies the following day.

ZZZZ

A large newspaper will contain about 100,000 words. If you read them all, your eyes would have traveled over half a mile.

Beat that!

If you live past 30 years old, your heart will have beaten over a billion times. It beats about 100,000 times every day.

INCREDIBLE!

Hairball horror

An 18-year-old visited the doctor complaining of stomach pains and vomiting—not surprising, after their investigations found a 10-pound hairball inside her. She had formed the hairball by eating her own hair over a period of years, and it filled nearly her whole stomach, measuring 15 inches by 7 inches. Gross!

Fastest finger first

The nails on your longest fingers grow the fastest, and all nails grow faster in summer than winter.

She's got it licked

Annika Irmler, a schoolgirl from Germany, has such a long tongue she can lick ice cream straight out of the bottom of a cone. Her tongue measures 3 inches.

Over-bite

Moving out? You could use a hand—or a mouth—from Jackie Del Rio from Illinois. He had such strong teeth and jaws that he could easily lift furniture with them. He was able to carry two tables and six chairs in this way!

Your hair can hold information about what you've eaten in the last six months.

Big foot

American actor Matthew McGrory, who died in 2005, had 17-inch-long feet, and needed

SIZE 29½ SNEAKERS.

It cost him up to $23,000 for a specially made pair of shoes! He was used to being supersized—when he left kindergarten he was already 5 feet tall!

BIG TOOTH

Everyone knows that your grown up teeth are bigger than your baby teeth—but it was still a shock for nine-year-old Mark Henry to watch his top right front tooth grow to an enormous one-inch long! The Canadian youngster had to have it taken out, and the dentist who removed it described the tooth as just "like a horse's!"

BRIGHT SPARK

A Romanian electrician named Constantin Craiu claims
he doesn't get electric shocks, even if he touches live wires.
He discovered this amazing ability while he was working,
thinking that the power was switched off. Since then,
"Electric Man" has shown the public how he can put wires
into a socket and use his hands to conduct the electricity
to turn on a lamp. He can even "charge" himself up
to cook fish in his hands.

DON'T TRY THIS AT HOME!

NEED A HAIRCUT?

How does your hair measure up...?

Sardar Pishora Singh from India has **eyebrow hair** that is 4 inches long.

Brian Peterkin-Vertanesian from Washington has a **single eyebrow hair** that has grown to over 6 inches in length.

Wesley Pemberton of Texas measured his **leg hair** in 2007; one of them was 6½ inches long.

Indian Radhakant Bajpal has **ear hair** that stretches 5¼ inches.

Badamsinh Juwansink Gurjar grew his **mustache** for 22 years, until it reached a length of 12½ feet.

Norway's Hans Langseth died in 1927 with a **beard** that measured 17½ feet.

AAATCHOO! A single sneeze stops your heart and other bodily functions—just for a moment.

CHOO!

FACING FACTS

Ripley's museums have some amazing wax heads on display. **Sara Disk Wearer**: Women of the Sara tribe in Africa would put wooden plates in their lips to make them unattractive to raiders. **Crocodile Man**: Bobby Blackburn from South Africa wore dentures made from real crocodile teeth! **Eye-popper**: Avelino Perez from Cuba could dislocate his eyes from their sockets. **Human Unicorn**: The Chinese man who had a 13-inch horn. **Wolf Man**: Larry Talbot was bitten by a wolf and gradually became one. **Lighthouse Man**: Using a 7-inch lighted candle he would light China's streets like a lantern.

SARA DISK WEARER

HUMAN UNICORN

EYE-POPPER

CROCODILE MAN

WOLF MAN

LIGHTHOUSE MAN

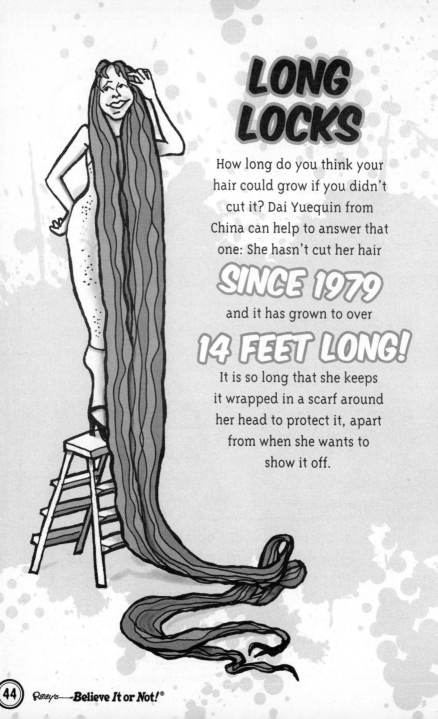

LONG LOCKS

How long do you think your hair could grow if you didn't cut it? Dai Yuequin from China can help to answer that one: She hasn't cut her hair

SINCE 1979

and it has grown to over

14 FEET LONG!

It is so long that she keeps it wrapped in a scarf around her head to protect it, apart from when she wants to show it off.

A deaf lady from Canada found that she could hear again after having surgery on her teeth in 1991.

No nose

Tycho Brahe from Denmark is famous for two very different reasons. Born in 1546, he was an excellent astronomer whose discoveries have helped shape our knowledge of the universe. He was also a bit of a fighter, and he had part of his nose

CHOPPED OFF IN A DUEL!

After this happened, he wore a false nose made of gold and silver. He stuck it in place with wax or putty.

Most parts of the body can repair themselves, as they are made of living tissue. The exception is a tooth, which is made of enamel.

Reclaimed youth

Granddaddy Reggie Myles from Scotland was 62 when he became ill with a genetic disorder. His gray hair fell out and he lost over

HALF HIS BODYWEIGHT.

However, with treatment, he regained weight and health, with the bonus side effects of losing his wrinkles and regrowing dark brown hair. Now he looks as young as his own kids!

Ripley's

CAREFUL CUTTING

DON'T TRY THIS AT HOME!

Need a haircut? Ansar Sheikh is a hairdresser with a difference—he holds the scissors in his mouth! He has performed haircuts like this in public for 24 hours at a time, but he ultimately wants to open a training school for other hairdressers. How will he explain what he's doing with scissors in his mouth? Carefully, we hope...

Ansar gets his tools ready for his next client...

LET'S TWIST AGAIN

Old age is no excuse for being stiff or having creaky bones. Martial arts expert Wang Jiangsheng from China is

83 YEARS OLD

and can still put his leg all the way behind his head.

and snips away while holding the scissors in his mouth...

creating the perfect cut. Another happy customer!

Can you touch your elbow with your tongue? Betcha can't... but it's not physically impossible for everyone, as proved by Nate Richard of Florida. His amazing 4-inch-long tongue can actually reach the elbow of his own arm.

Eye mites

Microscopic creatures known as follicle mites can

LIVE ON YOUR EYELIDS!

The creatures are white and shaped like bugs, but are way too small to see. Hundreds of them live at the roots of your lashes. Don't panic—they're harmless!

There are half a million sweat glands on your feet, and they can produce over a pint of sweat on a warm day.

SUPER SNORER

Next time you moan at your parents for their snoring, take pity on anyone within hearing range of Jenny Chapman. Her snores have been recorded at

111.6 DECIBELS!

That's louder than a jet aircraft! Jenny's ZZZZ's are noisy enough to drown out a truck or an express train speeding past!

TATTOO YOU

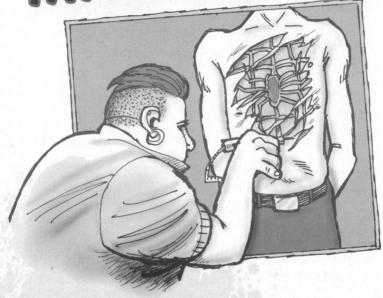

What's happened to this man's skin? Panic not—
his chest hasn't been scraped away to show off his
spidey-suit underneath. Instead, it's been tattooed to
look that way. The design is known as a

"TEAR OUT"

and was cleverly created by Dan Hazelton from Wisconsin.
It took ten hours to complete the whole thing.

Cell-by dates

Your body is made up of different types of cells: in
your blood, nerves, skin—everywhere. Each lasts a
different length of time before new cells replace it.

RED BLOOD CELLS

last three months, skin cells last only one month,
and bone marrow cells live for around only 12 hours.
Your nerve cells are super long-lasting: They stay
around for virtually your whole lifetime.

Maria Stelica from Romania suffers from
insomnia brought on by the death of her
mother. In 2003 she told doctors that she
had not slept for eight years.

Tasty fact

Not all of your taste buds are on your tongue.
Some are located underneath it, on your lips,
on the roof of your mouth, and inside your
cheeks. On average, a person has about
10,000 taste buds altogether.

Bumper jumper

What a job! Graham Butterfield is a professional bed tester, and he has to bounce on beds all day long to check their springiness and softness. He has his buttocks insured for $2 million, just in case they get damaged in the call of duty and he can no longer work.

BOING!

Adults have 206 bones in their body. Over half (106) of them are in the hands and feet.

Mountain life

People who live high up in the mountains have to cope with different conditions from those who live lower down. The air pressure is lower, so mountain dwellers have

EXTRA-LARGE LUNGS

to get the oxygen they need. They also have comparatively shorter arms and legs so their blood has less distance to travel around their body.

RIPLEY's
DANGEROUS DREAMS

A chef in Scotland has a distinctly dangerous habit—he cooks in his sleep! The sleepwalker is Robert Wood and he gets up several nights a week to cook fries, wok dishes, and even omelets, all without waking. He is now getting help from doctors to cure his habit—before he sets his house on fire!

BODY SHOCK...

Muscle power

At 21 years old, Aditya Dev is only 2 feet 9 inches tall, weighs just 22 pounds, and is famous for his bodybuilding. Nicknamed "Romeo," his trainer has made special 3-pound dumbbells to build up Dev's muscles properly without injuring himself.

Heads up

A human and a giraffe have the same number of neck bones: seven. A giraffe's neck is longer because the bones are longer.

AMAZING!

Robin Boyce from Washington state was born with nostrils the shape of hearts.

Medical marvel

Babies born too soon or too small have less chance of survival than bigger babies. It was thought that newborns under 14 ounces were too tiny to survive, but Amillia Sonja Taylor has proved that theory wrong. She was only 10 ounces when she was born in October 2006, and shorter than a ballpoint pen.

INCREDIBLE!

Days of old

Japan has over 40,000 people that are over 100 years old. Eighty-five percent of these are female.

Feeling blue

A man named Paul Karason has become famous for having blue skin! He decided to take large quantities of an old fashioned medicine called colloidal silver, and over the years it has totally changed his skin color. Some experts even think his insides might also have turned blue! Not surprisingly, the medicine is not recommended by doctors.

The human eye can recognize over seven million different colors, including more than 500 shades of gray.

Feeling healing

The Alabama doctor James T. Clack treated people in the 1940s, even though he was blind.

WOW!

Don't sweat it

Check your sweat—it can tell you what you've been eating. A man in China wondered why his sweat was green, and so were his bedclothes, underwear, and the water when he showered. Doctors finally figured out that Cheng Shunguo had eaten a cake colored with green clothes dye, instead of food dye.

ARCTIC ANTICS

Wim Hof is a man who likes to push his body to the limit by subjecting it to the coldest conditions possible. He has run a half marathon in the Arctic Circle, swum under the ice at the North Pole, and climbed to the "Death Zone" of

Mount Everest, each time wearing only shorts or swim trunks. He has also survived being buried in ice cubes up to his neck for over an hour. Wim says Tummo meditation helps to keep his body heat up.

BRRRRR!

A CUT ABOVE

Wear your hair to show you care: Indian cricket fan Bhola Sarder had his hair shaved and colored into a cricket picture to celebrate the Cricket World Cup in 2007. His

CRAZY

crewcut included the shapes of a bat and ball, an Indian flag, stumps, and a cricketer!

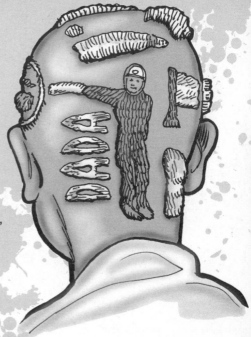

What blood type are you? Probably not H-H. It's the world's rarest blood type, and only about 50 people have it. All of them live in India.

Big baby

Leslie Bowles from Suffolk, England, weighed the same as an adult as he did when he was just three years old! Born in 1933, Leslie had grown to

142 POUNDS

by the age of three. He became known as the "ten stone baby."

PUMPED UP

A Ripley performer known as "Edema, the human automobile tire" used to put on shows where he used a tire pump to fill his stomach with air. His belly would inflate to three times its usual size! It's not such a strange thing these days: Surgeons sometimes pump up their patients in a similar way to make it easier to operate on them.

ALL SEWN UP

Professor Leo Kongee, alive in the 1930s, could sew buttons onto his body! He could even stitch them onto his tongue—

OWWWW!

He also performed in public, piercing his chest, cheeks, and ears with skewers.

Freaky feet

How far out can you twist your feet? Not as far as Raymond Gonzales, who has extra-flexible legs that allow his feet to turn completely backward. He's been able to twist his feet 180 degrees since he was a boy, and he thought it was normal until his mom saw him do it and freaked out.

SHARP THINKER

This has gotta hurt: Sarita Bista from western Nepal has been pulling pieces of glass out of her

FOREHEAD

since January 2006. Her doctors have no idea how the triangular-shaped fragments appear every day, and scans don't show any glass inside her skull. The poor

12-YEAR-OLD

actually faints sometimes when it happens, but it doesn't seem to be affecting her overall health.

SCISSOR SNACK

DON'T TRY THIS AT HOME!

Don't read this if you're squeamish... Lin Kong was picking at his teeth with a pair of scissors...

when his friend made him laugh—and he accidentally swallowed them!

The four-inch long scissors slipped down his throat. Doctors had to operate to get them out using only a local anesthetic...

as they feared that a general anesthetic would relax his throat muscles and make the scissors drop even farther down.

Going gray

When 11-year-old Rosemary Jacobs from Vermont visited the doctor over

50 YEARS AGO

she could never have foreseen that it would turn her gray. Not her hair, but her skin! The doctor prescribed nasal drops for her blocked-up nose. The drops contained

COLLOIDAL SILVER

which in large doses can turn human skin grayish-blue! Unsurprisingly, doctors don't prescribe it anymore.

SMILE!
You have just used a total of 17 face muscles. Much easier than being grumpy: It takes 43 muscles to frown.

In an average lifetime, a person will produce enough spit to fill two swimming pools. Gross!

Lucky ears

Thank goodness for big heads! A six-year-old boy in China slipped through the window bars, on the eighth floor, and could have fallen

60 FEET

if his ears had not become trapped in the bars because his head was so big!

Thick and thin

The largest artery in the body is the aorta, which transports blood from your heart. It is nearly as wide as a garden hose! The smallest blood vessels are the capillaries, which pass blood from the arteries into the veins, and these are about one-tenth the width of a single human hair.

EYE POPPING

What's the funniest face you can pull? It's probably good, but not as good as the one Jalisa Mae Thompson from New Jersey can pull. Since she was nine she's been able to pop her eyeballs so they look like they're coming right out of their sockets! Add a peculiar rolling tongue, and it's no surprise she won the 2006 Ripley's Funny Face Contest!

LEOPARD MAN

Tom Leppard from Scotland has skin like no other person on earth: He's had it tattooed with leopard skin print! Nearly every inch of his body has the tattoos of a leopard's spots. Only the insides of his ears and the skin between his toes are left blank.

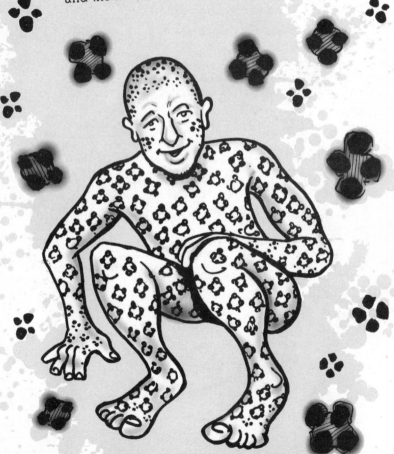

Take a look around

Martin Joe Laurelio was known as the "Human Owl" as he could twist his neck 180 degrees (half a circle) to look behind him. He was born with extremely flexible body parts, and he practiced to make himself even more bendy.

Impulses travel along your nerves to your brain at 170 mph, as fast as a sports car.

Chew or cough?

Have pity for poor Nicholas Peake, a lecturer from England who just can't stop coughing. He coughs up to

100 TIMES EVERY HOUR,

and has done this for the last 15 years. That's over

A MILLION

coughs! The only thing that seems to stop the coughing is chewing gum—and Nicholas hates gum.

It would take over a million mosquitoes to drink all of a human's blood.

PEOPLE POWER...

Fancy footwork
Martha Morris was born in the U.S.A. in the 1900s, and became famous as the "armless wonder." Despite having no arms from birth, and legs that ended below the hips, Martha could write, draw, sew, knit, and type—all with her toes.

AMAZING!

Your jaw muscles are strong enough to bite with a force of 160 pounds (roughly 35 house bricks)—that's about half as hard as a Rottweiler.

Pump up the volume
Your heart will pump enough blood in your lifetime to fill more than three supertankers: about a million barrels.

Baby boom
When a baby is born, it grows about 20 times bigger to become a full-size adult. Before it is born, it has grown six BILLION times! That takes it from teeny tiny egg to a fully formed baby in its mother's womb.

BILLIONS!

Brainbox

A normal human brain weighs around 50 ounces—roughly the same as seven packs of cookies (YUM!). Baron Georges Cuvier, an 18th-century scientist, was brainier than most. His brain weighed an amazing 64 ounces.

YUM!

Hic! Hic!

Spare a thought for Charles Osborne from Iowa, who hiccuped for 58 years of his life. He managed to live a relatively normal life, even fathering eight children. The hiccups finally stopped in 1990.

Got a sniffle? Try this 19th-century remedy: Sniff a dirty sock nine times to cure your cold!

No spitting please

When you talk, almost invisible drops of water spray out of your mouth—as many as two drops in any word you say.

UGH!

Soap stars

The average human body contains enough fat to make seven bars of soap, and enough water to fill a 10-gallon tank.

Eye, eye!

Twins in the U.S.A. have identical birthmarks in their eyes. Shirley Santos has an arrowhead-shaped mark in the iris of her right eye and her brother has the exact same mark in the iris of her left eye.

Zhang Quan from China can clap at 107 decibels, which is nearly as loud as a helicopter.

RIPLEY's
PLEASE DON'T CRY

Imagine how you'd feel if tears streamed down your face whenever you ate or drank... that's what life's been like for Patricia Webster from England for nearly 20 years.

CARELESS CUTTING

Toshie Kawakami from Japan has an extreeeeeeeemely long eyebrow hair! It measures nearly

7 INCHES

and she tucks it behind her ear to keep it out of her eyes. Unfortunately, her hairdresser accidentally cut it, but it grows so fast (about a ½ inch each month), it was soon back to "normal."

She has a rare condition that links her saliva cells to her tear glands, making her sob when she chews and swallows. Fortunately, it's been found that botox injections can cure the crying and make her appear happy again.

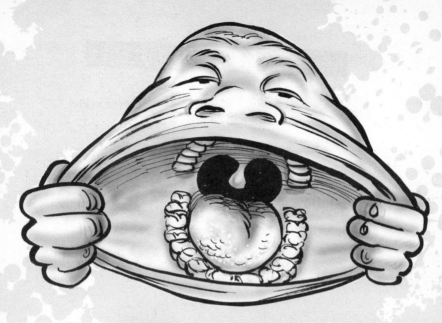

BIG MOUTH

And the winner is... Francisco Domingo Joaquim!
He beat other big-mouthed competitors in Rome by
stretching his lips around a

11-OZ SODA CAN
—SIDEWAYS!

The other entrants were wide-mouthed with admiration,
after they only managed to wrap their chops around
coffee cups, beer bottles, and saucers—which still
sounds quite large, don't you think?

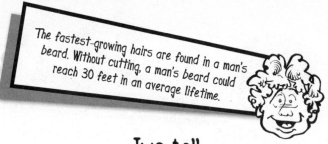

The fastest-growing hairs are found in a man's beard. Without cutting, a man's beard could reach 30 feet in an average lifetime.

Two tall

The tallest man on record was Robert Wadlow from Illinois. He was 8 feet 11 inches tall and still growing when he died in 1940. Not far behind him was Missouri's Ella Ewing, who at 8 feet 4 inches was the tallest women in the world alive at that time.

All fingers and toes

Counting has never been easier than for father and son Albert and Karl Perculeza from the Philippines. Both of them have extra fingers and toes, making a grand total of 48 digits between them! Each has

12 FINGERS

(including thumbs), and 12 toes, and all of them work properly like any other digit.

The average blink rate for a person is 25 times a minute, which adds up to more than 13 million blinks a year.

STABBING PAINS

Luis Zarate was taken to the doctor in his Peruvian hometown, after complaining of severe stomach pains. It's no surprise—his stomach was full of

METAL

items that he had eaten. Scans showed nails, a knife, screws, barbed wire, bolts, and pens: A total of 17 metallic items!

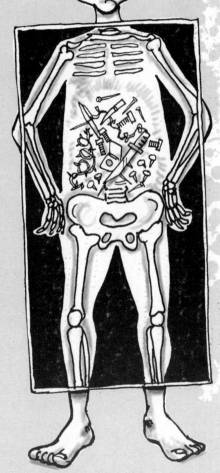

The lifespan of the average eyelash is about 150 days—then it falls out.

USB FINGER

Jerry Jalava always has the information he needs at his fingertips—literally. He lost half of one finger in a motorcycle accident and had to have a false finger made. He customized it to suit his profession as a computer engineer, and had a memory stick put in under the nail. That's handy!

Both feet in... that's a good start.

Right, let's just get comfortable.

Ooh, a paperclip! Better get rid of that to make more room.

Now then, how do I close the lid behind me?

Wu Xizi, a Chinese contortionist, squeezed his whole body into a 23 x 11 x 15 inch box — even though he is 67 inches tall!

LET ME OUT!

Shiyuan shampoo

Eighty-year-old Luo Shiyuan from China needed 12 members of his family and friends to help him wash his hair! The major event took place in 2006 and was the first time in 26 years that he'd had a hairwash. He had also gone many years without cutting his hair, so it had grown to 6 feet 6 inches long.

Your body is a mixture of different substances making up your cells. One substance is iron, and there's enough of it in a human to melt down and make a medium-sized nail!

Living and breathing

You take about 600 million breaths in a lifetime—about

breaths every day. When you breathe out, you lose droplets of water vapor adding up to around 2 pints each day, or a watering can-full each week.

BELIEVE IT OR NOT?

Eighteenth-century doctors were fooled for a while when a maidservant called Mary Toft convinced the world she had given birth to baby rabbits! She was watched over by a midwife named John Howard, who confirmed she had gone into labor and produced rabbits.

Doctors were fascinated and came up with all sorts of theories—and then Mary confessed that it was all a scam.

X-RAY EYES

Natalia Demkin from Russia claims to have an
extremely unusual talent: X-ray vision. She looks

INSIDE OTHER PEOPLE'S BODIES

and tells doctors what is wrong with them, from
cysts and tumors to metal plates that have been
added by surgeons. She has performed several
tests to see how successful she is, and many remain
unconvinced about her powers, but others are
blown away by what she does.

WRITE ON

Zhang Yongyang from China can touch his nose with his tongue. You might think that's not that unusual–you may be able to do it yourself–but he's taken it a big step further and learned to use his tongue for drawing and writing!

Zhang has a very long tongue that he can touch his nose with...

but he prefers to dip it into ink then write and draw with it...

creating beautiful Chinese characters! Now that's clever!

BIG HAIR

Walking through doorways could cause problems for Aaron Studham, who styles his hair into a giant mohawk. It adds

20 INCHES

to his height and takes him about an hour to get it to stay that way.

Around 100 hairs on your head fall out and are replaced EVERY DAY!

I ♥ BURRITOS

Jamie Sherman from Arizona just loves Mexican food. That's not so strange, except she hated it until she had a heart

TRANSPLANT

in 2001. It seems that her organ donor, Scott Phillips, adored Mexican cuisine, and she had inherited his cravings along with his heart.

A man in Sweden had his hearing restored in 1995, when doctors operated to remove a 47-year-old bus ticket stuck in his ear!

TUG OF WAR

Super-strength martial arts expert Dan Netherland of Tennessee can keep his fingers gripped together while ten people link at either side of him to try to pull his hands apart.

It can take only 20 seconds for a red blood cell to make its way around your body.

Ripley's——Believe It or Not!®

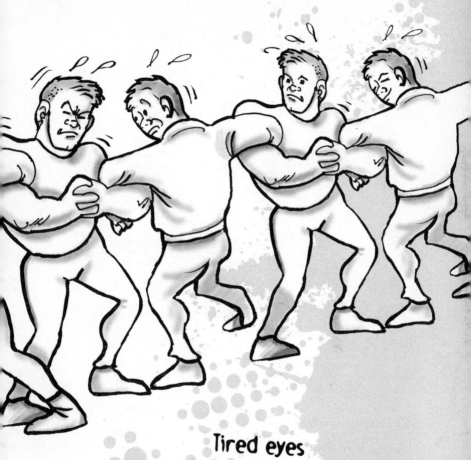

Tired eyes

Bernt Aune from Norway had problems with his right eye and needed a cornea transplant. In 1958, he received the cornea from a 73-year-old body and was told it should help him see for five more years. Bernt has had the cornea ever since, making the eye part more than

125 YEARS OLD!

SUCKER!

You may know that snakes can dislocate their jaw to fit in a supersized meal—and that's exactly what Marco Hort from Switzerland does as his party trick. Except instead of swallowing tasty treats like rats and birds, Marco manages to fit

264 DRINKING STRAWS

into his overlarge mouth.

Susan Marchich from Chicago woke up one day with no hair left on her head. It was all there when she went to sleep, but it had totally fallen out the next morning.

GOOD NIGHT'S SLEEP?

A 19-year-old Frenchman fell asleep on a railway track. He was sleeping face-down between the tracks when a high-speed TGV train drove right over the top of him—and he survived! These trains travel at speeds of over 160 mph, but still the teenager didn't wake up as it hurtled toward him.

ZZZZzzz

BANANA-GEORGE

George Blair, born in 1915, is famous: He is Banana George, the world's oldest barefoot water skier, and he makes his presence known with his trademark yellow wetsuits and bright yellow boat.

He fell in love with waterskiing
when he was 40 and has been
doing it ever since. Not satisfied with
extreme summer sports, he also took up
snowboarding at age 75, drove his first
racing car at 81, and did his first
parachute jump at 82!

INCREDIBLE BODIES...

Super vision

You don't need to be a superhero to have great vision—
your eyes are amazing anyway. On a clear, moonless
night, with a high vantage point (like a mountain), your
eyes can see the flame of a match that is 50 miles away.

Circus act

WOW!

People are always fascinated by the
world's tallest and shortest people. One 1930s circus
act featured tiny Mary Schmidt, who measured 3 feet
5 inches tall, alongside giant Jim Tarven, who was 7 feet
11 inches. As well as the 4 foot 6 inches difference in their
height, he weighed over 4½ times more than she did.

Margrette Klever was such a hairy baby that at just six weeks old, she had shoulder-length hair.

Pleased to see you

A restaurant in Beijing was staffed by smiling faces,
both front and back: The waiters had smiles shaved into
their hair to attract customers.

Dreamtime

A dream commonly lasts up to 20 seconds, but as we have nearly 1,500 each year, that adds up to five full-length movies' worth!

Nightmare nails

The fingernails on Li Jianping's left hand are an astonishing 3 feet 3 inches long in total. He has left them to grow for 15 years, but has to sleep on his left wrist to keep his hand still through the night. He doesn't like to move in crowds, either, for fear of breaking the nails.

> Blood travels 12,000 miles a day— the same as driving across the U.S.A. four times.

Surprise surprise!

Peep into Kylee Hodgson's baby carriage and you'll get a bit of a shock: Her twin girls have completely different skin! Remee is white and Kian is black, but both have the same father. Doctors say it is very rare, but it is possible for twins from mixed-race parents to inherit either the black or the white genes and to look different.

VULCAN BLOOD

Canadian doctor Alana Flexman was astonished to see green blood when she operated on one of her patients. The doctor described the blood as the color of avocado skin, and later found out it had turned green because her patient had taken too much headache medication.

Each inch of a human armpit has over half a million bacteria!

Ugh!

The average birth weight of a baby is a little under 8 pounds. Italian baby Fedele, born in 1955, weighed three times that—an incredible 22 pounds!

Off and on

Here's weird: Californian Brenda Sheklian acts like a human light switch. She says that her body has electrical powers that turn off the TV, freeze her computer, and make lightbulbs blow. She also claims that street lamps turn off as she walks past, and back on again afterward when she's farther down the street!

FOOD FOR THOUGHT

DON'T TRY THIS AT HOME!

The World Stinging Nettle Eating Championship of 2010, held in England, saw Sam Cunningham win the title after he

ATE 74 FEET OF NETTLES

in one hour. The competitors eat the freshly picked stinging plants raw, and must keep their mouth wet to stop it from swelling. The nettle stings can affect the tongue so badly it turns black—yikes!

RIPLEY's
POWERFUL PONYTAIL

Shailendra Roy from India can pull trucks, cars, trains, and buses with his hair! He strengthens his hair with mustard oil and braids it into a ponytail before hooking it to heavy items and pulling them behind him. In May 2008 he pulled a train weighing more than 40 tons!

Try playing snap in the Indian village of Kodinhi. It has six times more twins than the average around the world. That's 250 sets of twins from just 2,000 families.

Dead or alive?

Doctors had to defend themselves BIG TIME after declaring their patient was

DEAD—FOUR TIMES!

Dona Ramona from Colombia kept slipping into a diabetic coma, and each time she did this her doctors said she was dead. Thank goodness they didn't bury her—as she made a full recovery every time!

Over 650 years ago, an artificial limb was made for Scotland's king, Robert the Bruce. It was an iron hand, complete with moving fingers.

A knock to your "funny bone" feels so weird because the nerves in your elbow run very close to your skin.

Your body produces half a gallon of gas a day, in burps and farts!

THE SHAME!
A blush spreads across your skin, but also makes your stomach lining redder.

If you could peel an adult's skin and stretch it out, it would measure between 16 to 22 square feet.

The lens of your eye is the only internal body part that grows your entire life.

It takes just 0.02 of a second for your brain to realize when you have dropped a book on your toe!